SAMURAI

LOUIE STOWELL

ILLUSTRATED BY JASON ENGLE

History consultant: Dr. Stephen Turnbull, Leeds University

Reading consultant: Alison Kelly,
Roehampton University

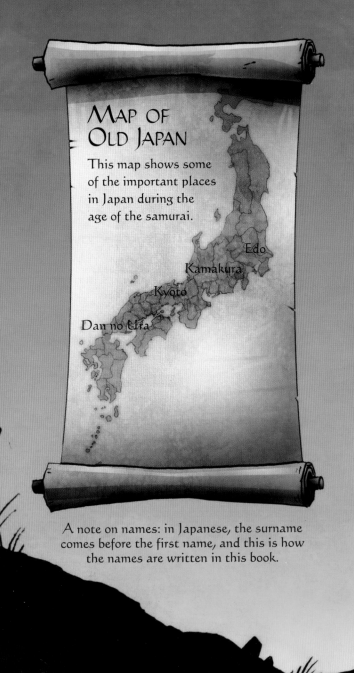

MAP OF OLD JAPAN

This map shows some of the important places in Japan during the age of the samurai.

Edo

Kamakura

Kyoto

Dan no Ura

A note on names: in Japanese, the surname comes before the first name, and this is how the names are written in this book.

CONTENTS

Chapter 1
Death or Glory

In old Japan, there lived a special type of horseback warrior, known as a samurai. Samurai warriors were fierce, fearless... and trained to hack their enemies to pieces without a second thought. You wouldn't want to meet one on the battlefield...

Off the battlefield, it was another story.
Samurai warriors weren't thugs. They lived by
a strict moral code, just like the knights who
lived in Europe at the time. Most of them were
highly cultured and courteous men – and they
looked impressive too, in their elaborate
battlegear and fearsome face masks.

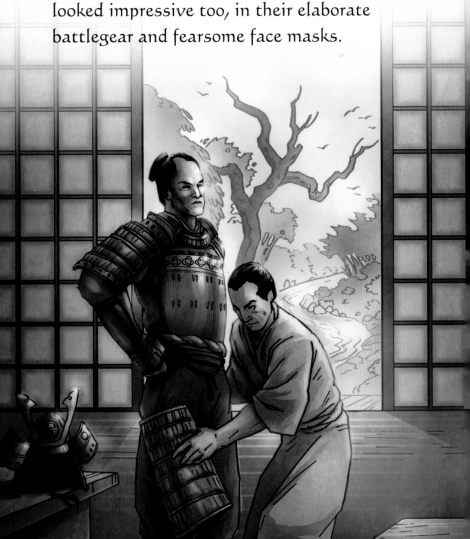

Many of these warriors came from rich, powerful families, and the samurai title was handed down from father to son. Ordinary foot soldiers from poor backgrounds occasionally rose up to join this warrior elite – if they fought with outstanding bravery, or if they married the daughter of a samurai – but it was pretty rare.

Although they had servants, samurai didn't expect to be pampered. Feasting on rich food or living in a luxurious home was looked down on, because it showed that you were soft and self-indulgent.

In fact, the samurai moral code required warriors to live lives of service and obedience. The earliest samurai, who lived in around the 10th century, worked for the emperor. Some guarded his palace, in the city of Kyoto, while others defended remote villages from bandits and pirates. People believed the emperor was descended from the ancient gods of Japan, but that didn't mean his divine blood gave him special powers.

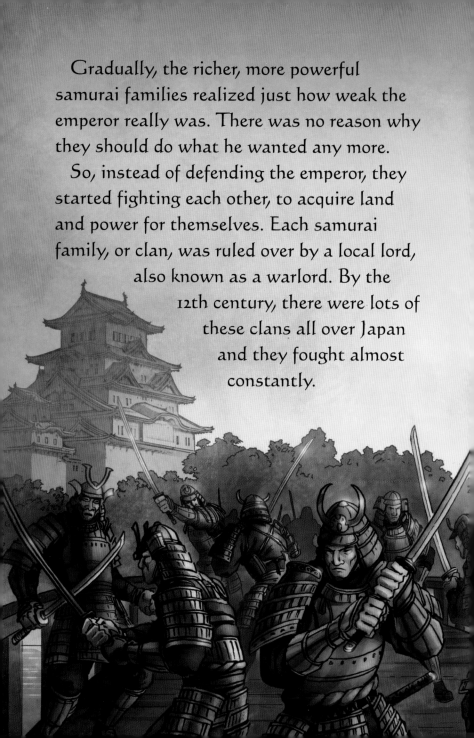

Gradually, the richer, more powerful samurai families realized just how weak the emperor really was. There was no reason why they should do what he wanted any more.

So, instead of defending the emperor, they started fighting each other, to acquire land and power for themselves. Each samurai family, or clan, was ruled over by a local lord, also known as a warlord. By the 12th century, there were lots of these clans all over Japan and they fought almost constantly.

Most of Japan is too hilly to farm on, and in those days fertile fields were very valuable. Everyone wanted as much land as they could possibly lay their hands on.

It was a samurai's job to defend his lord's lands and win him even more by fighting with other clans. He had to swear an oath to be loyal for the rest of his life, and to be ready to fight at all times. Loyalty to your lord meant more than life itself.

If a samurai had to choose between protecting his lord from an attacking army, or saving his own wife and children, there was no contest. He had to let his family die.

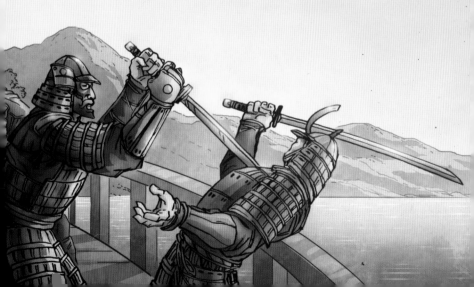

A warrior's own life mattered even less, and samurai were trained from an early age to feel no fear in the face of death.

The one thing that they were afraid of, though, was being thought of as a coward. There was nothing worse than being beaten in a battle then living to tell the sorry tale. If your side looked as if it was losing, there was only one thing to do: kill yourself.

Samurai were expected to commit ritual suicide, known as seppuku, rather than face the shame and humiliation of being captured.

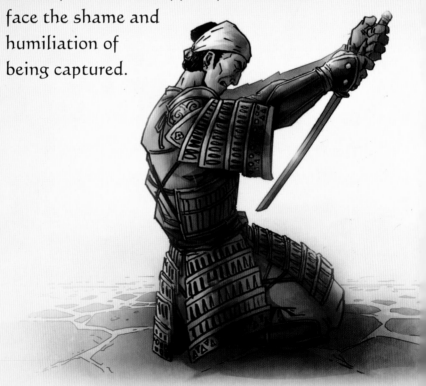

CHAPTER 2

SAMURAI SKILLS

Warriors usually began their training as children. Some learned their trade by serving as pages in the castle of a lord, others picked up their fighting skills from older, more experienced family members.

The traditional image of a samurai is of a man wielding an elegant sword, or drawing back the string of a bamboo bow. But, in the heat of battle, warriors had to use any means they could to take down an enemy.

Young samurai were trained in every possible military tactic. They learned how to fight well with a blade and how to fire arrows on horseback with deadly accuracy. But they also picked up dirtier tricks, such as how to slice open an enemy's throat with a dagger at close range, or fight off an attacker with their bare hands, and then throttle him to death.

Both girls and boys were taught how to fight, and some girls even became famous warriors. One woman, named Tomoe Gozen, was a legendary archer and sword-fighter, who commanded troops of samurai in battle.

But women couldn't officially become samurai, and most of them used their training to defend their homes.

When a boy from a samurai family was between 13 and 17 years of age, he had a coming-of-age ceremony known as a genpuku. During this, he took a new name, shaved his forehead and received his first proper sword.

Afterwards, he went to war side by side with the older samurai. It wasn't unheard of for a teenager to become an army general. When they weren't fighting battles, warriors played a sport named yabusame – basically archery on horseback. The rider had to focus on aiming his arrow at a wooden target and letting go of the string at exactly the right moment, at the same time as staying firmly in the saddle and guiding the horse.

Doing all these things at once trained warriors to be tremendously agile, and sharpened their mental powers too. The most deadly samurai fought with their wits, hearts and souls, as well as their physical strength.

Warriors also played a violent sport called inu o-mono. In this game, wild dogs were trapped in a pen and the contestant had to ride around, killing all the dogs using as few arrows as possible. It was even trickier than yabusame, but a better preparation for battle. The dogs were fast-moving and unpredictable just like enemy warriors on horseback.

Samurai learned how to fight with swords using hefty, sword-shaped wooden sticks called bokuto. These could inflict a lot of damage on an unwary opponent.

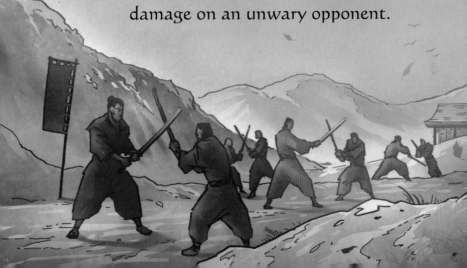

One forceful blow with a bokuto could break a man's arm. At best, young samurai usually limped away from their training sessions covered in angry bruises.

Adult samurai wore two swords – even in peace time – as a sign of status. (Ordinary soldiers were allowed only one.) The longer katana was a curved, two-handed blade, used for cutting and slicing. The shorter wakizashi (which means "side arm") was for stabbing at close range.

Samurai often gave their swords names and treated them with great respect. A warlord named Tokugawa Ieyasu even declared that a samurai's sword was his soul. Warlords hired master craftsmen to equip their samurai with weapons, and the finest blades were deadly works of art.

The most famous swordsmith in Japan was a man named Masamune, who lived about 700 years ago. Masamune invented a new way of forging katana that made them incredibly hard and tough.

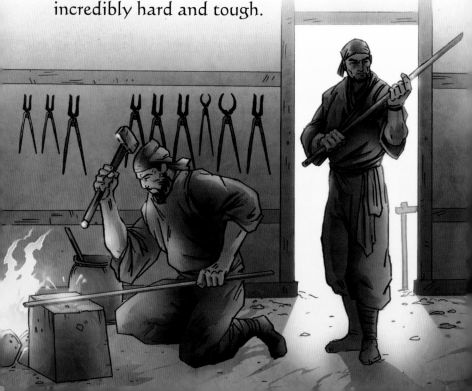

When the metal for the sword was molten-hot, he would fold the blade over and over, banging it flat as he went.

Blades made in this style were famously sharp. One legend tells of a samurai who was able to commit seppuku by cutting off his own head.

Swordsmiths usually tested newly forged swords on bundles of bamboo. But there were more unpleasant methods too. Sometimes, new swords were tried out on piles of corpses: a well-crafted blade could slice through up to seven bodies.

Samurai were even permitted to test their own swords on condemned criminals, although not many warriors actually went that far.

But fighting was not a
samurai's only purpose in life. There
is an ancient Japanese saying, which
goes "pen and sword in accord." The ideal
samurai was supposed to be able to write
poetry and appreciate art and music, too.
   Some warriors wrote poems before going
into battle. It was a chance to say goodbye
to the world and to prepare the mind
for death.

CHAPTER 3

THE SCARLET SEA

A thousand years ago, Japan was a dangerous place to be. The country was locked in a bloody war between the mightiest of the samurai families – the Taira and the Minamoto clans. They were fighting over who should control the emperor's court... and ultimately, all of Japan.

As the clans fought, whoever was winning the war put their own chosen emperor on the throne.

In 1180, the Taira army was the strongest of the two. Their leader, Kiyomori, forced the old emperor to resign and put his own grandson on the throne instead. The new emperor, Antoku, was only a year old, but in those days it was quite common for a child to become emperor. It made it easy for Kiyomori to control him, too.

Kiyomori died soon after and his son Munemori took over as lord of the clan. This was bad news for the Taira. Munemori was weak compared to his father. In 1183, the Minamoto chased him and the rest of the Taira clan out of Kyoto, including the young emperor Antoku.

The Minamoto made Antoku's younger half-brother, Go Toba, the new emperor. Still, the Taira didn't give up, and the war raged on. Year after year, the hiss of arrows and the clash of swords echoed through the towns and over the boggy rice fields of Japan. Slowly, but surely, the Taira were pushed back, all the way to the ocean.

On April 25th, 1185, the two armies met at sea for their final battle. It was a fresh spring morning in the bay of Dan no Ura, and the air was tangy with salt. The 850-strong Minamoto fleet was lined up in the bay, with all their boats bobbing side by side.

Facing them, the 500 Taira ships were grouped into three squadrons. Tomomori, Munemori's younger brother, took command of the Taira fleet. He was an excellent sailor and knew that stretch of sea very well.

The women and children of the Taira clan huddled behind their warrior men on board the ships. Battle yells went up on both sides, rising to a deafening roar. Over the din, Tomomori bellowed, "Our enemies know nothing of war at sea. We'll take them down, one by one... and throw them into the ocean!" He gave the signal and a flock of whirring arrows sped towards the enemy. Men screamed in pain as the missiles met their targets. The Minamoto archers fired an answering volley.

"Don't think about your lives!" cried Tomomori, as some of his men cowered low.

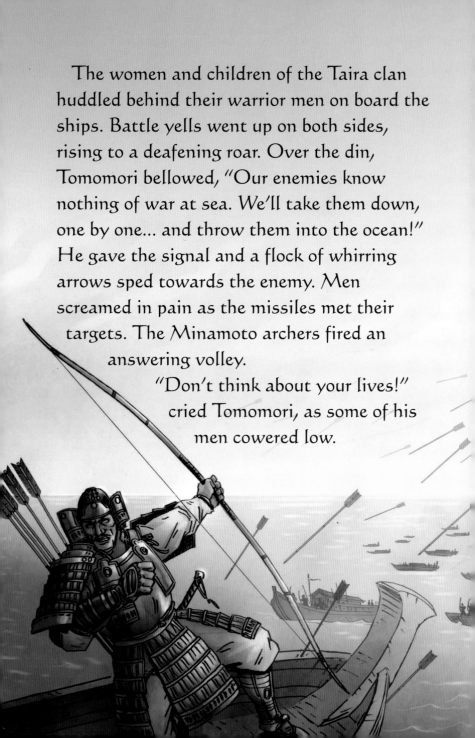

On the deck of one of the smaller Taira ships stood six-year-old Antoku. The little emperor ducked down on the creaking deck to avoid a fresh rain of arrows. Then, he peeked over the side. Hundreds of enemy ships, bristling with warriors, were spread along the horizon.
They were getting closer and closer.

The two fleets met in the middle of the bay. Hundreds of Taira warriors streamed on board the Minamoto vessels, their swords and daggers at the ready. A brutal hand-to-hand struggle began, spreading from ship to ship, until the decks flowed with blood.

Thanks to Tomomori's skilled seamanship, the Taira vessels managed to surround the Minamoto's larger fleet.

"Well done, Tomomori! We've got them," crowed Munemori. "We're going to win!"

But they had a traitor in their midst. Suddenly, one of the Taira captains turned his ship and attacked his own fleet. He sent word to the Minamoto general, Yoshitsune, telling him exactly where to find the young emperor. As the Minamoto archers picked off the Taira oarsmen and the men at the helm, the Taira ships were sent spinning out of control.

Antoku's grandmother, who was on board ship with him, realized that it was only a matter of time before they would be captured. She turned to the warriors who surrounded her – samurai who had sworn to protect her and the little emperor. "I won't be taken by the enemy," she announced, boldly. "I will leave with the emperor. Who will follow me?"

Then she took Antoku
firmly by the hand and started
to walk to the edge of the ship.

Antoku looked up at her,
wide-eyed.

"Where are we going,
Grandmother?"

She hugged him tightly.

"We will have a city
under the waves,"
she sobbed.

Now the emperor
understood. He
was dizzy with fear,
but his grandmother
had always taught him
that duty mattered above
everything else. So
together they leaped
into the swirling water
and sank down into
the darkness below.

The rest of the battle was swift and brutal. Feeling that all hope was lost, many of the Taira samurai followed their emperor into the sea. In despair, Tomomori tied an anchor around his ankle to weigh him down, and threw himself into the churning waves.

But Munemori could not bring himself to jump, even though he was supposed to be setting an example as the lord of the clan. His mother, who was on board with him, was disgusted with her cowardly child. She yelled curses at him as he gripped the rail of the ship.

"You're the son of an umbrella salesman!" she spat.

"I can't jump," Munemori cried, staring in a panic at the thrashing waves.

Then, one of his samurai gave their lord a shove and he toppled overboard with a scream. His son jumped in after him.

More and more Taira warriors, women and children flung themselves into the sea, or were thrown from the ships by the triumphant Minamoto.

As they did so, something strange began to happen... the sea slowly changed from murky green to vivid red. The dye from the Taira banners, and the blood of the fallen warriors, had stained the water scarlet.

Chapter 4

The First Shogun

By the end of that day, the Minamoto clan had won the battle, and the war. General Yoshitsune, their captain, rounded up the Taira survivors, including a dripping wet and shame-faced Munemori and his son. An eagle-eyed Minamoto warrior had spotted them trying to swim away and fished them out of the sea with a rake.

Yoshitsune led his captives through Kyoto to the court of the emperor. Although people jeered, many secretly felt sad to see noble warriors brought so low. But the prisoners did not have to suffer this disgrace for long: They were all executed.

Yoshitsune was handsome and popular, and he'd already won lots of battles. Now he was seen as even more of a hero. When he arrived at Kyoto in triumph, the young emperor's courtiers showered him with praise and gifts.

But his elder brother Yoritomo was bitterly jealous. Yoritomo was the lord of the Minamoto clan, but he was terrified that Yoshitsune would try to take over now. So he accused his brother of being a traitor and sent men to capture and kill him.

Yoshitsune went on the run, with his old friend Benkei at his side. Benkei was a Buddhist monk, but also a great warrior. Some say he was a giant, too. Together they dodged Yoritomo's men for several years. But, in June 1189, they were finally cornered in a mountain fortress.

No one knows for sure what happened next – Yoshitsune has had so many fantastical stories written about him that fact and fiction have blurred. According to some tales, loyal Benkei held off their attackers until the very last minute, even though he had so many arrows sticking out of him that he looked like a porcupine. This gave Yoshitsune the chance to commit seppuku and avoid a shameful death.

But, according to another version, they both escaped to Mongolia, a land near China. There, Yoshitsune became known as Genghis Khan, a great emperor who conquered much of Asia. Whatever really happened, Yoritomo got rid of his rival once and for all.

Three years later, in 1192, the emperor gave Yoritomo the title of shogun. This was an ancient title that used to be granted to generals who served their emperor well. But now it meant that Yoritomo was in charge, and the emperor was merely a puppet.

Yoritomo set up his own government in the town of Kamakura and named it the bakufu – or tent government – after the curtained area where a general would sit before a battle. He wanted to make it clear that he was a military leader, with thousands of warriors to back him up, and not a toothless emperor.

All the lords of the samurai clans had to swear an oath to be loyal to the shogun, but in their own lands they were free to run things as they liked.

Yoritomo's rule was brief. In 1198, after only seven years as shogun, he had a terrible riding accident. Some said his horse was startled by the angry ghost of his brother Yoshitsune. He died from his injuries the following year.

Many of the shoguns who ruled after him didn't last long either. After Yoritomo's death, the title of shogun was passed on from father to son. But there was often a younger brother or cousin, or a lord from another powerful clan, who was ready to go to war to steal the title for himself.

An attack from China in 1274 forced the squabbling samurai to put aside their differences, at least for a while, to fight their common enemy. That year, a fleet of ships sailed towards the Japanese coast.

On board were about 20,000 fearsome Mongolian and Korean warriors led by Kublai Khan, grandson of the mighty Genghis Khan.

They were armed to the teeth with weapons that were more advanced than anything the samurai used. Their bows could shoot further and pierce tough metal, and they even had very basic bombs.

But, bad weather at sea forced the Mongol fleet back. They returned seven years later with even more troops.

This time, as they attacked, the fleet was smashed to pieces by a typhoon that seemed to come from nowhere. People called it kamikaze, meaning "divine winds" – because it seemed like a miracle. Japan was safe now... from outside threats, at least.

Not all samurai were happy to be governed by a shogun, and some still believed the emperor should be in charge. In 1333, a group of rebel samurai managed to defeat the shogun and put Emperor Go Daigo on the throne, as the one and only ruler of Japan.

They were led by a cunning warrior named Kusunoki Masashige. He was a brilliant military strategist, full of clever plans and tricks. When the shogun's supporters fought back, Masashige advised the emperor to retreat to the hills and fight their enemies from there. But the emperor wouldn't listen.

"I won't retreat!" he cried, stubbornly. "You must face the enemy in battle now!"

Masashige bowed his head and loyally accepted his master's foolish command. He wrote a poem of farewell and left it with his teenage son, Masatsura.

On a baking hot afternoon, Masashige rode out of the gates of Kyoto with a general who was loyal to the emperor, and a small band of men.

They met their enemy beside the
Minatogawa river. Masashige looked out
grimly at the forest of enemy spears, glinting
in the sun, as far as the eye could see.

"For the divine emperor!" he bellowed, as
he spurred his horse on to meet them. The
enemy surged forward too. Masashige felt
the blade of a katana bite into his thigh. But
he fought on bravely.

Before long, he was wounded in eleven
places, and couldn't fight any longer.
He pulled out his dagger and cried out,
"I wish I had seven lives to give for
my country!" then stabbed
himself in the stomach.

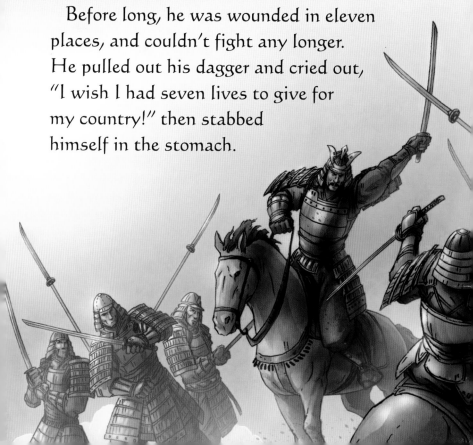

Young Masatsura had sworn an oath to his father that he would fight to the death for Go Daigo. The emperor never regained his throne, but Masatsura was still able to keep his promise.

It was the evening before a battle in 1348 and he was meditating in a Buddhist temple. Suddenly, he knew with perfect clarity that he was going to die very soon. So he took an arrow with an iron head and cut a farewell poem into the wood of the temple door. A few days later, he died defending the cause of the emperor.

CHAPTER 5

FAMOUS WARLORDS

Samurai who died bravely for a hopeless cause, like Masashige and his son, are often heaped with praise in Japanese stories and legends. Brave losers were remembered with awe and respect, for putting loyalty before victory.

But most samurai still preferred to win their battles, whatever it took. This was especially true of some of the most famous samurai warlords, who stopped at nothing in their lust for power.

In the 1400s, the local warlords grew so powerful that the shoguns could no longer control them. The result was a bloody, all-out war between the clan lords, that lasted for about 150 years – between the 1460s and the very early 1600s. This came to be known as "the time of warring states" – or the Sengoku Jidai.

All this chaos made it possible for an ambitious warrior to rise to the very top.

Oda Nobunaga, the son of a minor warlord, was born in 1534, in Shobata Castle, in the region of Owari. He didn't seem like the sort of child who would grow up to achieve great things. As a boy he was so strange and rude that he earned the nickname, Owari's Great Fool.

He designed his own garish clothes and liked to walk along munching noisily on a piece of melon, then spitting the seeds out all over the place. This was considered outrageous, especially for the son of a lord.

When he was fifteen, his father died, and Nobunaga behaved disgracefully at the funeral. He took a handful of the ceremonial incense and hurled it at the vase which contained his father's ashes.

Nobunaga was a brave fighter, but he showed no interest in taking care of his dead father's lands and warriors. His tutor, Hirate Kyrohide, wrote a letter to Nobunaga, pouring out his feelings of disappointment and pleading with him to change his ways. Then he committed a special kind of seppuku, known as kanshi, which meant suicide as a protest against the actions of your lord.

Nobunaga was so shocked and moved by
this that he was inspired to stop fooling
around and to make something of himself.
After building a temple in memory of his
dead tutor, he set himself a huge challenge.
His ambition was to become the mightiest
warlord in all of Japan.

But first he had to get his
own family properly under
control. Both his brothers
were plotting against him.
So he killed one of them
and pardoned the other.

Next, Nobunaga set out to fight and beat as many other warlords as he could. Perhaps he was still a bit of a fool and a dreamer, to take on so many mighty enemies. But, although he lost a few battles, he won a lot more. Field by field, castle by castle, he conquered all the lands around him. He killed the lords who lived there and forced their samurai to work for him instead – although some proud samurai committed seppuku rather than submit to him.

By 1559, all of the Owari region was his, and he allied himself with other clan leaders, making him even more powerful.

But, in 1560, Imagawa Yoshimoto, another mighty warlord who lived nearby, rose up to challenge Nobunaga. He gathered a vast army of between 20,000 and 40,000 men. Some of these soldiers were mounted samurai, but the rest were lowly foot soldiers, known as ashigaru. Warlords had started to rely heavily on these rough and ready fighting men during the Sengoku Jidai.

Yoshimoto's forces invaded Nobunaga's territory and destroyed two of the castles on the borders of his lands. Furious, Nobunaga sent out a scouting party to find out more. Yoshimoto's men had pitched camp for the night in a little wooded valley. Silently, the scouts listened to the drunken shouts and singing, as the army celebrated its victory. They rushed back to tell their lord the news.

Nobunaga only had time to raise a small army of a few thousand men. But he decided to fight Yoshimoto's army anyway, even though he was outnumbered ten to one.

Since it was his own land, Nobunaga knew every ditch and hillock of the terrain where Yoshimoto's men were camped out, so he knew just the place where his own men could hide.

One stifling morning, as Nobunaga put his attack plan in motion, Yoshimoto's guards were nodding off at their posts.

Under cover of a summer thunderstorm, he launched a clever ambush. Nobunaga's men streamed out from under the trees, scattering their enemies in every direction. They succeeded in killing Yoshimoto and kidnapping or slaughtering most of his gigantic army.

Nobunaga and the other warlords often employed a special kind of warrior to carry out sneak attacks. These warriors were known as ninja, and their world was one of secrets and shadows.

Ninja dressed in black and used a fighting style known as ninjutsu, which means " the art of stealth" in Japanese.

44

They were notorious for being able to slip into well-guarded places without being seen, which made them very useful as assassins and spies.

But, the warlords often used less subtle methods of attack, including a devastating new foreign weapon that had recently arrived in Japan: the gun.

Samurai had been using very basic guns since traders from China first brought them over in 1510. But, in 1543, shipwrecked Portuguese merchants brought in a new type of gun, known as an arquebus.

Arquebuses were much more effective than the guns that had been used before. They were more accurate and easier to carry, although they were slow to load.

Many skilled swordsmiths started to become gunsmiths instead, and Nobunaga and other warlords placed large orders. At first, Nobunaga didn't know how to deal with the fact that arquebuses were slow to reload. A troop of enemy archers could pick off a line of arquebus marksmen before they had a chance to fire a second round.

He discovered the answer from his most hated enemies – the warrior monks. In Japan at the time, many Buddhist monks were also skilled warriors. Nobunaga felt that his position of power was threatened by these fierce fighting men and tried to wipe them out.

In 1570, when he attacked a monastery in the hills, his army was greeted with volley after volley of gunfire from 3,000 arquebus-toting monks. "How are they firing so fast?" Nobunaga wondered. Then he noticed that the monks were standing several rows deep, which meant that one row of arquebus marksmen could fire while the next row slotted bullets into their guns.

In 1575, Nobunaga had a chance to try this out for himself. A warlord named Takeda Katsuyori laid siege to one of his most important castles. When Nobunaga arrived at the scene, he brought a troop of ashigaru with him, all armed with arquebuses. He lined them up three deep behind a wall and ordered the first row to fire.

Then they dropped back and reloaded as the next row came forward to launch a new volley. Katsuyori's troops were blown to pieces.

Through luck, military skill and brutality, Nobunaga grew more and more powerful. He massacred most of the warrior monks and snatched the lands of warlord after warlord. He couldn't be a shogun because he wasn't descended from the Minamoto clan – the original shoguns – but he started using a personal seal which read: tenka fubu. This means "one realm under one sword" – and there was no doubt as to whose sword he meant.

Although he was now a mighty leader, Nobunaga never shook off his crude manners. He often teased his samurai for being ugly, bad at poetry, or clumsy in battle.

Towards the end of his life, Nobunaga had a bitter quarrel with one of his finest samurai warriors, Akechi Mitsuhide, and in 1582, Mitsuhide betrayed him. He ambushed Nobunaga in a temple, and forced him to commit seppuku.

But Mitsuhide only had a few days to enjoy his triumph. One of Nobunaga's generals, Toyotomo Hideyoshi, slaughtered the traitor and his little army within a single week, and took power himself.

Hideyoshi couldn't become shogun, either, because he was only the son of a poor farmer, who had risen to become a samurai commander through skill and hard work. Instead, he took the title of taiko, which translates roughly as prime minister.

One of the first things he did with his new rank was to stop other men from rising from a lowly status to a position of power. He also banned anyone who was not a samurai from carrying weapons. So only men from noble families could fight in wars.

Hideyoshi was short and ugly – Nobunaga had given him the cruel nickname of "monkey" because of his looks. But, despite his rough exterior, he was a highly cultured man, fond of writing poetry. He spent vast sums of money building beautiful castles, and became fascinated with a ritual from China known as the tea ceremony. This was an extraordinarily complicated, elegant way of making and drinking cups of green tea.

Hideyoshi helped make it popular all over the country, and people in modern Japan still perform this slow, beautiful ritual.

Hideyoshi died in 1598, leaving his five-year-old son as the ruler of Japan. A number of adult regents were really in charge, but they were no match for an old ally of Nobunaga's, a warlord named Tokugawa Ieyasu.

Since Hideyoshi's death, Ieyasu had been very busy. He'd made alliances with other warlords and recruited teams of highly skilled ninja spies into his service. When he felt that his forces were strong enough, Ieyasu declared war on the regents.

Before long, Japan was in a state of all-out war once again. But, this time, when peace came, it lasted for hundreds of years. Ieyasu, who was descended from the Minamoto family, emerged as the victor.

In 1603, he received the title of shogun, with the emperor's blessing. There was no one left to challenge his power. Japan was now one nation under one ruler and Nobunaga's dream had come true – even if he didn't survive long enough to enjoy it.

CHAPTER 6

SAMURAI AT PEACE

When Tokugawa Ieyasu became shogun, it was the beginning of the end for the samurai. His warlords and their men had done their job almost too well. They had defeated all their enemies.

This peaceful time came to be known as the Edo period, named after Edo, the new capital – the city we now call Tokyo. A thriving, bustling place, Edo had a population of over a million by the 1700s, making it the largest city in the world.

This was great news for merchants, traders and shopkeepers, who had an endless supply of customers. But lots of samurai were out of a job, now that there was hardly any fighting to be done. Their lords had become government officials, and samurai had to take boring desk jobs to earn their living.

To stop bored samurai from causing trouble, Ieyasu ruled the country with an iron fist. He had spies everywhere and kept careful track of everything his samurai subjects did – from where they lived to who they married.

Some samurai were determined to keep the old ways alive, even if there were no more glorious wars to fight in. One of the greatest samurai heroes, Miyamoto Musashi, lived during the Edo period. He never pledged himself to a lord, although he did fight in a few of the rare battles that happened during his lifetime.

Musashi was a ronin, or wave man – that meant someone who is tossed about on the seas of fate and has no duty to anyone but himself. A samurai usually became a ronin if his lord died. But some men, like Musashi, chose that path on purpose. He went on a musha-shugyo, or warrior pilgrimage, to improve his combat skills by fighting duels with other samurai along the way.

Musashi won his first duel when he was only 13 years old. He fought a much older warrior, using only a wooden training weapon, a bokuto, while his opponent had a proper metal sword.

Thrilled with this victory, Musashi set off from his village and tramped from town to town, picking fights. He was a strange-looking man, with diseased skin and no interest in his appearance.

All he cared about was combat. As soon as he'd beaten one opponent, he was on the lookout for another.

Later in life, when his health grew poor, he retired to a monastery and wrote books teaching others how to fight.

After his death, all kinds of legends grew up around this lonely figure. Some even said that he fought against mythical creatures known as nues. These evil beasts were said to have monkeys' heads, tigers' legs and tails like writhing, hissing snakes.

Although lots of samurai were bored and unhappy, at least the peace and quiet gave them a chance to write books about what it meant to be a warrior. If they hadn't, their noble thoughts and daring deeds might have been forgotten. Samurai authors started to use the term bushido – the way of the warrior – to describe the moral code that samurai had been living by for centuries.

One samurai named Yamamoto Tsunetomo wrote, "The way of the warrior is found in death." He advised samurai to meditate every day on all the violent ways a person can die – from falling off a cliff to being struck by lightning – so that they wouldn't lose their warrior spirit.

But life remained calm and dull, and the grip of the government grew even tighter. In 1639, Ieyasu's grandson, the shogun Iemitsu, decreed that visitors from Europe would be banned. Then, for almost 200 years, Japan was cut off from the rest of the world in a peaceful bubble. The samurai were trapped inside.

CHAPTER 7

THE LAST SAMURAI

On Friday, July 8th, 1853, a cluster of excited fishermen were standing on the seashore near their village, close to Edo, staring at something across the bay.

"Dragons!" cried one of the men. "Look, they're puffing out smoke!"

Sure enough, smoke was rising on the horizon. It seemed to be coming from three huge black shapes that were getting steadily closer. Were they under attack by monsters?

"Don't be ridiculous!" someone else cried. "They're foreign ships... and they're on fire!"

The black ships were steamboats and they belonged to the US Navy. These American warships had come to force Japan to open up its borders and start trading with the outside world once again.

The shogun didn't want to agree to this, but his advisors went behind his back and made a deal with the Americans. They felt they had no choice. The foreigners had much better guns and cannons, and the samurai had been living in peace for so long that they weren't ready to fight such a powerful foe.

The shogun resigned soon afterwards and a government made up of ambitious politicians replaced the old military bakufu. They put a new emperor on the throne, giving him a bigger role in running the country than an emperor had had for hundreds of years.

The government also made it illegal for anyone who wasn't in the army to carry arms. Without wars to fight and swords at their sides, samurai warriors effectively ceased to exist.

But the samurai spirit didn't die out entirely. During the Second World War, some Japanese pilots went on suicide missions, dive-bombing enemy ships. They became known as kamikaze pilots, after the winds that had saved Japan from the Mongol invaders all those years ago.

These pilots still believed in the samurai ideal... that the way of the warrior lies in death.

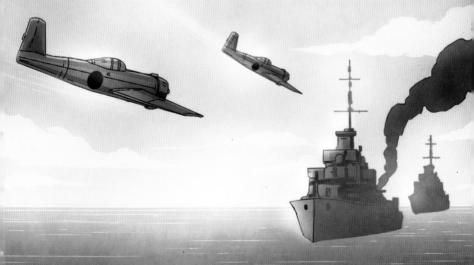

SAMURAI TIMELINE

Around 900-1000 Samurai warriors start off by working for the emperor, but then begin fighting amongst themselves.

1185 The Minamoto clan defeats the Taira clan at Dan no Ura.

1192 Yoritomo, leader of the Minamoto, becomes the first shogun.

1274 and **1281** A Mongol fleet attacks Japan, but the Japanese defeat it... with help from the weather!

1333 Samurai warriors overthrow the shogun and put Go Daigo on the throne, but they are defeated soon after.

1460s-1600s A period of bloody fighting between warlords, known as the Sengoku Jidai, or period of warring states.

1534 The birth of Oda Nobunaga who later becomes a powerful warlord.

1582 Nobunaga is betrayed and forced to commit seppuku by one of his own samurai. Soon, Toyotomo Hideyoshi becomes the ruler of Japan.

1603 Tokugawa Ieyasu becomes shogun and the Edo period begins.

1639 Visitors from Europe are banned from Japan.

1853 American ships arrive in Japan and force the shogun to allow traders from all over the world to enter Japan.

1860s An emperor is restored to the throne and samurai are banned from carrying swords, bringing the age of the samurai to a close.

Index

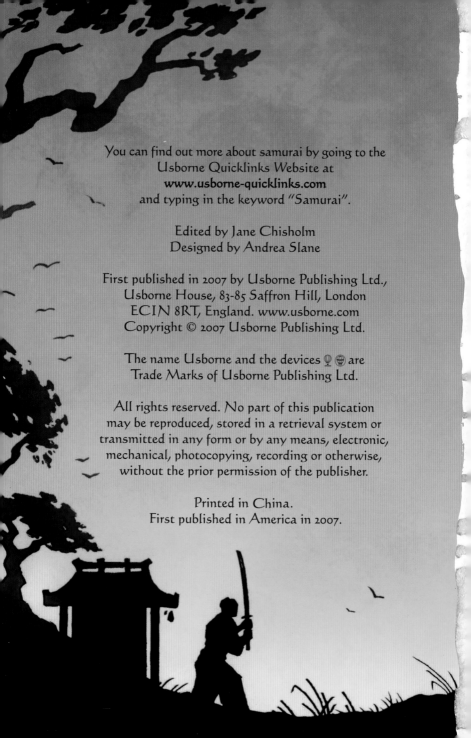

You can find out more about samurai by going to the
Usborne Quicklinks Website at
www.usborne-quicklinks.com
and typing in the keyword "Samurai".

Edited by Jane Chisholm
Designed by Andrea Slane

First published in 2007 by Usborne Publishing Ltd.,
Usborne House, 83-85 Saffron Hill, London
ECIN 8RT, England. www.usborne.com
Copyright © 2007 Usborne Publishing Ltd.

Printed in China.
First published in America in 2007.